SHANGO
and the
AMAZING Magical
NO WORRIES
Spell

Simon Menzies

ISBN-13: 978-1539134466
ISBN- 10: 1539134466

Books in the Shango Series:

- **Sleep** – Shango and the Amazing Magical Sleeping Spell

- **Anxiety** - Shango and the Amazing Magical No Worries Spell

- **Anger** - Shango and the Amazing Magical Calming Spell

- **Fear and Phobias** - Shango and the Amazing Magical Bravery Spell

- **Confidence** - Shango and the Amazing Magical Confidence Spell

PLEASE READ CAREFULLY BEFORE USING THIS PRODUCT

This Book may cause drowsiness or sleep in the reader or unintended listeners.

Do not listen to this book while driving or operating machinery. Do not read this book within hearing of someone driving or operating machinery. When reading or listening to this book, choose an environment that is quiet and safe.

Results will vary, each individual will respond differently. We do not claim that there are typical results that all consumers will generally achieve. A small percentage of listeners might be impervious to suggestion and some will accept suggestion faster than others. There are no guarantees that reading or listening to this product will help or resolve specific issues. We take no responsibility for how the listener will respond.

This product is not intended to replace medical treatment. Consult with your Doctor/Physician on all medical issues regarding your child's condition and treatment. The content is not intended to be a substitute for professional medical advice, diagnosis, or treatment. It is not a substitute for a medical examination, nor does it replace the need for services provided by medical professionals. Always seek the advice of your medical professional before making any changes to treatment.

For best results, please follow the Advice and Instructions to Reader. If you encounter problems, the Audio version will provide a controlled rendition of the story and might be more effective. The more the story is repeated, the more effective it will be.

The child must be able to understand the vocabulary used in the story.

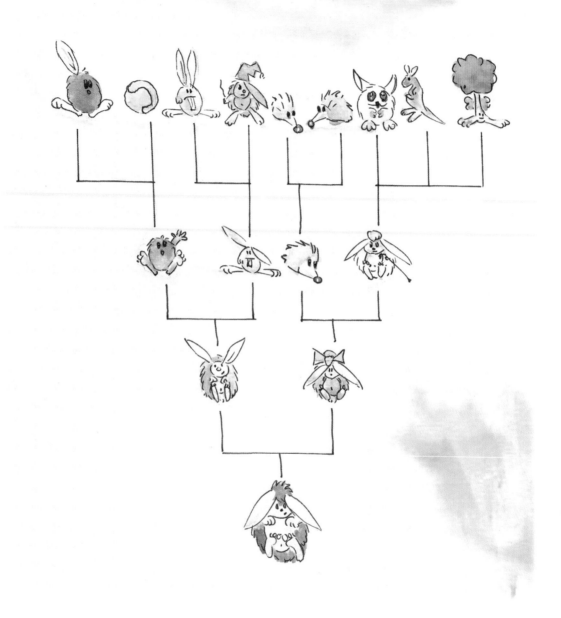

Shango's Family Tree

Advice and Instructions to Reader

You can read the story using the word 'worry' currently in the text or substitute it with the child's specific issue in the blank spaces provided. If you choose to use the current text, explain to the child prior to reading the story that when the word 'worry' is used, it means their special issue. It should also be explained to the child that some worry can be good and perfectly normal to help avoid danger, resolve problems or improve performance, but should be in moderation and rational.

If your child has difficulty getting to sleep, then please refer to 'Shango and the Amazing Magical Sleeping Spell' first. This book will be more effective once the child is sleeping more easily.

To improve fluency, please read through the story before reading it to the child.

Use a slow, gentle, rhythmic voice. It may sound silly, but it works.

Emphasize the words in **bold**, with a slow and deliberate tone.

Ensure the child is comfortably in bed and ready to listen before starting.

For the first few times, complete the story EVEN if the child falls asleep before the ending. They will still be able to hear you.

Follow the instructions in bracketed sections [_____], for example [YAWN].

On the last page of the book you will have two options to end on: one is to continue sleeping, the other to continue napping (daytime).

The story uses Positive Suggestion and Repetition to influence the child. It may read oddly, but the language is intentional.

Much of the effectiveness of this book depends on a positive connection between child and reader as well as the reading technique explained above. Some may find the CD/Audio version more effective.

After the first reading of the book, the following day or after waking up, please encourage the child to create their own illustrations of their Shango and Dream World. This is a part of the process of connecting the child to the story and will make the story even more effective on following nights.

Please persevere - The more often the story is read, the more effective it will be.

SHANGO and the Amazing Magical No Worries Spell

Shango is a funny little thing and sometimes not. He is bigger than a ladybug and smaller than an elephant and sometimes not. Shango is about the same age as you, perhaps a 100 years older or a 100 years younger, or perhaps not.

Shango is a Tidbog and Tidbogs are relatives of tree-wongles, hedgehogs, bunnies, hamsters, monkeybugs, fizzbogs and a whole bunch of other things.

Shango is a very **calm and happy** thing and he **never worries** when he does **not need to worry**, but Shango was not always **calm and happy** like he is now. He often worried [about _____] until he was given the Tidbog Wizard's, known as Wizbogs, Amazing Magical **No Worries** Spell by his cousin Wolly-Bee. But more about that later......

When Tidbogs are awake they live in our imaginations, but when they **go to sleep** they live in a magical **Dream World**.

Tidbogs can take on many different shapes when they are asleep, but when awake they are fluffy and round and sometimes not, with two big eyes, sometimes three, and two big ears, sometimes one, and they can see and hear everything.

Shango lives in a place called Windybottom, so called because it's at the bottom of a windy valley, so they say.

There are lots of Tidbogs, like the Pongalot Tidbogs of Cowpat fields, where you can pat the cows in the fields, so they say. Shango's family are called the Tootberry Tidbogs and for now we are only interested in them and especially in Shango.

No-one knows why the Pongalot Tidbogs pong a lot, BUT the Tootberry Tidbogs earned their name because they like to eat tootberries, which are made of bath bubbles and magic and something else. Tootberries make **you feel very, very sleepy** and some scientists think they are the cause of the high winds in Windybottom, so they say.

Tidbogs prefer to live underground in a magical place, where they **can sleep safely** and have dreaming adventures. Their dreams are real. When they **sleep** they can do magical things and help their special friends, children like you. Each Tidbog has his own special friend and ALL Tidbogs have magical powers.

Because Shango is a young Tidbog he has not found his special friend until now. Shango **loves you.** He wants you to be his special friend.

Wolly-Bee Tidbog from Ozzz being photobombed by a Koala.

Tidbogs **like to sleep** very much. When they **go to sleep**, they travel to a magical place of dreams where anything can happen, whatever **you** want. They can change shape and colour and even be invisible and they can play and **be happy or just sleep deeply**. This is why they like to go to sleep. [YAWN.]

Shango is a clever Tidbog and he knows that it is **normal to worry about some things** sometimes because it helps him to be careful or to fix the worry so he does **not worry anymore** [and he especially knows not to worry about _____]. He also knows **not to worry too much**, because too much worry is not good for him and **being happy** is much more fun.

As mentioned at the beginning of our story, Shango **stopped worrying** about all sorts of things when his cousin Wolly-Bee Tidbog, from a place called Ozzz, told him about the Wizbog's Amazing Magical **No Worries** Spell.

Shango's cousin Wolly-Bee is **happy and calm** and does **not worry** about things he does **not need to worry** about.

When Shango used the **No Worries** spell he **stopped worrying** and now he wants to share it with you so you can **stop worrying** [about _____] too.

Shango's Amazing Magical **No Worries** Spell works best of all when your eyes are closed and **you go to sleep**. You can see him much better when **you close your eyes**. Even if you are not tired, you can still close your eyes and use your amazing imagination.

Like you, Shango is very special. When **you close your eyes** you will begin on a **magical journey** with Shango. All you have to do is **close your eyes** and start imagining.

When you hear Shango's **NO WORRIES** spell, you will go on an **amazing adventure** with him very soon and, just like magic, you will wake up **happy** and with **no more Worries**; all you have to do is follow what Shango says.

Shango is **feeling very sleepy now** and he wants to go to the **Dream World** and give you his magical **No Worries** spell.

Shango wants you to join on an adventure in the Dream World and **stop worrying** like Shango?

That makes Shango **VERY happy**.

Where is SHANGO?

Now for the magic bit:

Shango says you have to blink your eyes three times now [CHILD TO BLINK 3 TIMES], then **keep your eyes closed** and whisper very slowly and quietly the Tidbog magic word **FIZZBALLS** [CHILD TO SAY 'FIZZBALLS'] and your magical journey can begin.

Shango wants you to keep your eyes closed, **do not worry about anything** and just concentrate on my voice.

Shango says you have to breathe in deeply and when you breathe out slowly, you will notice your **whole body relaxing** and starting to **feel very tired and sleepy**.

[VISIBLY/AUDIBLY BREATHE IN DEEPLY AND THEN SLOWLY OUT IN TIME WITH THE CHILD.]

Well done, that is perfect. Keep breathing in deeply and as you breathe out, your whole body becomes **more and more sleepy**. Very good.

Let your **whole body relax** more and more with each breath and just think about Shango and my voice.

You now feel very sleepy and you want to go with Shango to the **Dream World**. You are doing very well.

[KEEP BREATHING DEEPLY AND ENCOURAGING THE CHILD TO RELAX UNTIL YOU FEEL IT APPROPRIATE TO MOVE ON.]

Shango now wants you to see or imagine 10 steps in front of you going down to the **Dream World**. Well done. In a moment, Shango wants you to follow him down the steps. And when **you go down deeper and deeper,** you will hear me count each step from 10 all the way down to 1, and **you will go all the way down** into Shango's **Dream World** where **you will feel safe and happy.** [YAWN.]

[COUNT DOWN SLOWLY WITH A PAUSE BETWEEN NUMBERS, GETTING QUIETER WITH EACH NUMBER.]

Now you see the steps in front of you, I will start to count you down them, one by one:

10 - you are going down the steps

9 - you are feeling very sleepy

8 - down deeper and deeper to the Dream World

7 - deeper to sleep

6 - sleepier and sleepier

5 - keep going down

4 - down, down to the Dream World

3 - deeper to sleep

2 - you are now very sleepy

1 - you are now asleep.

Well done. You have entered Shango's **Dream World** and soon you can **go on a magical adventure** with Shango.

Shango says just listen to my voice and **do not worry** about any other noises or thoughts. Any familiar noises and every word I say will just help you **go to sleep** more and more.

Shango knows you have a **wonderful imagination** like him. In Shango's magical **Dream World** whatever you imagine is real, but **only good and happy** things.

Shango now wants you to imagine a wonderful place where **you feel very happy and safe**. It can be a memory or somewhere real or a new special place you have invented. It is up to you.

Nod your head when you are in your special place where **you feel happy and safe**. [WAIT FOR THE CHILD TO NOD.]

Shango now wants you to notice, when you think about the **wonderful place** you are now in, that the **happy feeling you now have** inside you gets bigger and bigger. The more you think about **the happy feeling** the more and **more happy you feel**.

Shango wants you to know now that whenever you think of Shango or hear his name, **even** when you are awake, this **wonderful happy feeling** will come back to you, **even bigger** than it is now.

If you think of Shango's name now you will notice the **feeling of happiness** gets bigger and bigger inside you.

You are doing **very well** and this makes Shango **very happy**. Shango **loves you** and he knows **you love** Him.

What colour is your Dream World Shango?

Now Shango wants to give you the magic of **No Worries**.

Shango holds your hand [GENTLY HOLD THE CHILD'S HAND] and smiles a **big, happy smile**. He whispers the **magic** word **Fizzballs** and you now feel his magical power flowing from his hand over to you like a **wonderfu**l stream of light filling you up inside. Your hand is getting warmer as you feel all his **No Worries** magic coming though to you. You are now **feeling very happy** and filling all the way up to the top of your head with **No Worries** and **happiness**. Well done. The spell is working. Notice how **happy you feel.** You **now feel very calm and happy**.

Shango wants to test your new '**No Worries'** power. Shango wants you to imagine or to see you are now holding a big red balloon in front of you, floating in the air. The balloon is full of your worry [of_____].

Shango now wants you to let the balloon full of your worries go and watch it float away. You see the balloon getting smaller and smaller and as it does your worry gets smaller and smaller also, as it floats away into the distance and disappears.

Nod your head when the balloon with all your worry has disappeared. [WAIT FOR THE CHILD TO NOD]. Well done.

You now feel very calm and happy and you now know that your worry [about_____] has **gone forever** and if you have any more worry in the future you can just think of Shango and **you will feel happy and loved.**

This wonderful feeling of being **calm and happy** you now have inside you will stay with you when you wake up and every day you will **be more and more happy.**

You are doing very well and this makes Shango **very happy**. He will now **always be with you to help you.**

Granny Gangapants thinks you are amazing. Can you draw her something?

Night-time Story Ending

After your adventure with Shango, **you will sleep very well** and you will wake up normally and easily in the morning feeling **very happy and loved**.

You know Shango is now with you always and whenever you think of Shango he will make **you feel very happy and loved**.

Next time, when you go down Shango's 10 steps to the Dream World **you will go to sleep** very quickly and easily and 10 times sleepier than you are now.

You will always love hearing Shango's story and you will look forward to going on more wonderful adventures with Shango in the **Dream World**.

If you hear me leaving the room or any other familiar noises, they will just help **you sleep more**.

You can now go on a wonderful adventure with Shango into the **Dream World** where you feel happy and loved and sleep very well until the morning when you will wake up with **no more worries**.

Sleep now…...

Please draw Shango something?

Daytime Nap Story Ending

You want to sleep now and have a wonderful dreaming adventure with Shango. **You will sleep very well** and when you hear familiar noises around you, **you will go to sleep** deeper and deeper into the **Dream World**.

Next time, when you go down Shango's 10 steps to the **Dream World**, you will **go to sleep** very quickly and easily and 10 times deeper than you are now.

You do not worry [about _____] any more and you will look forward to bedtime and going to Shango's Dream World again.

After you have had a **good sleep**, you will wake up when your name is said and you will feel **very happy and loved**, but now **you just want to sleep** and have a lovely dream time with Shango.

Sleep now......

[WHEN NAP TIME IS OVER, YOU CAN WAKE THE CHILD UP BY SAYING THE CHILD'S NAME CLEARLY AND FIRMLY. ALLOW THE CHILD A FEW MINUTES TO WAKE UP FULLY – AND TO REMAIN POSITIVE AND HAPPY.]

Can you draw this Fizzbog some magic stuff?

Please draw one of your dream friends for Monkeybug?

This Wizbog wants to see your Dream World.

Can you draw Bunny something?

Draw happy Shango what's in your Dream World?

Draw Monkeybug your Dream World?

BOOM!